Science

What's the Difference?
Butterflies
and Moths

by Lisa M. Herrington

Content Consultant
Dr. Lucy Spelman

Reading Consultant
Jeanne M. Clidas, Ph.D.
Reading Specialist

Children's Press®
An Imprint of Scholastic Inc.

Library of Congress Cataloging-in-Publication Data

Herrington, Lisa M., author.
  Butterflies and moths / by Lisa M. Herrington.
    pages cm. -- (Rookie read-about science. What's the difference)
  Summary: "Introduces the reader to butterflies and moths"-- Provided by publisher.
  ISBN 978-0-531-21485-5 (library binding) -- ISBN 978-0-531-21533-3 (pbk.)
1. Butterflies--Juvenile literature. 2. Moths--Juvenile literature. 3. Children's questions and answers. I. Title.

QL544.2.H4635 2016
595.78--dc23   2015017322

Produced by Spooky Cheetah Press
Design by Keith Plechaty

Printed in China 62

1 2 3 4 5 6 7 8 9 10 R 25 24 23 22 21 20 19 18 17 16

Photographs ©: cover left: Athipat Chumnanpa/Shutterstock, Inc.; cover right: Grzegorz Gust/Dreamstime; 3 top left: Panachai Cherdchucheep/Shutterstock, Inc.; 3 top right: Mikhail Melnikov/Shutterstock, Inc.; 3 bottom left: Iscatel/Shutterstock, Inc.; 3 bottom right: Cristian Gusa/Shutterstock, Inc.; 4 top: mshch/Thinkstock; 4 bottom: heibaihui/Thinkstock; 7 top: mshch/Thinkstock; 7 top background: a454/Shutterstock, Inc.; 7 bottom: heibaihui/Thinkstock; 7 bottom background: Wang Wentong/Shutterstock, Inc.; 8: Jens Stolt/Dreamstime; 11: Dr. John Brackenbury/Science Source; 12: Yarek Gora/Dreamstime; 15: Paul Harcourt Davies/Nature Picture Library; 16: Bornin54/Dreamstime; 19: Schwab Lukas/Prisma/Superstock, Inc.; 20: Calin Tatu/Dreamstime; 23: Viter8/Dreamstime; 24: Noradoa/Shutterstock, Inc.; 25 top: Danita Delimont/Getty Images; 25 bottom: Matee Nuserm/Shutterstock, Inc.; 26: Wolfgang Kaehler/Superstock, Inc.; 27: Cristian Gusa/Shutterstock, Inc.; 28 left: Bill Bouton/ARKive; 28 right, 29: Gary Scott/Thinkstock; 30: Scubaponnie/Dreamstime; 31 top: Schwab Lukas/Prisma /Superstock, Inc.; 31 center top: Jens Stolt/Dreamstime; 31 center bottom: Yarek Gora/Dreamstime; 31 bottom: Dr. John Brackenbury/Science Source.

Map by XNR Productions, Inc.

Table of Contents

Which Is Which?

They both have four wings. They flutter when they fly. They also have **antennas** and six legs. But which is the butterfly and which is the moth?

Did you guess right? Butterflies and moths are a lot alike. But they are not exactly the same. There are ways to tell them apart.

FUN FACT!

There are about 20,000 kinds of butterflies. There are more than 160,000 types of moths.

butterfly

antennas

wings

moth

7

Day or Night Fliers?

What is an easy way to tell a butterfly from a moth? Butterflies fly mostly during the day. They flutter from flower to flower to drink **nectar**. Most butterflies are not active at night.

Most moths are **nocturnal**. They come out at night. They rest during the day. You may spot them flying near a porch light in the dark. They are often attracted to the light.

Like butterflies, some moths drink nectar from flowers. Other moths do not eat at all.

Wonderful Wings

Most butterflies have bright, colorful wings. They sometimes blend in with flowers. This helps the butterflies stay safe from birds, spiders, and other animals. Bright colors also warn enemies that some butterflies taste bad!

When butterflies rest, they close their wings.

Moth wings are often brown or gray. They can blend in on tree trunks or brown leaves. They hide from the animals that eat them, such as bats, owls, and bears.

Moths rest with their wings open.

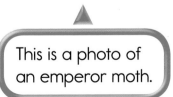

This is a photo of
an emperor moth.

head

thorax

abdomen

Different Bodies

Butterflies and moths are **insects**. Like all insects, they have three main body parts. Those are the head, thorax, and abdomen. But the bodies of butterflies and moths are not exactly the same.

Butterflies have long, thin bodies.

Look at the long, thin body of this golden helicon butterfly.

The scales on a moth's body look like thick hair. They help keep the moth warm.

This male oak eggar moth has a furry body.

Tuned In to Antennas

Both butterflies and moths have antennas on their heads. They use them to feel and smell.

Most butterflies have skinny antennas with round knobs at the ends.

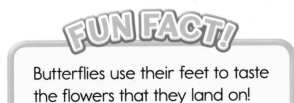

FUN FACT!

Butterflies use their feet to taste the flowers that they land on!

Most moths have antennas that are short and feathery. They do not have knobs at the tips.

Now you know the difference between these insect look-alikes!

This giant peacock moth has feathery antennas.

Butterflies and Moths

Butterflies and moths live around the world. They do not make their homes at the North or South Pole. It is too cold there.

North America

South America

MAP KEY

Range of butterflies and moths

Each fall, millions of monarch butterflies make a long journey from Canada and the United States. They migrate, or travel, south to Mexico to stay warm for the winter.

The Chinese luna moth has no mouthparts, so it can't eat. It lives for only about a week.

Europe

Asia

Africa

Australia

The pellucid (pel-OO-sid) hawk moth is found in Africa, India, Southeast Asia, and Australia. It has see-through wings.

Antarctica

long, skinny antennas with knobs at the ends

bright, colorful wings

long, thin body

butterfly

That's

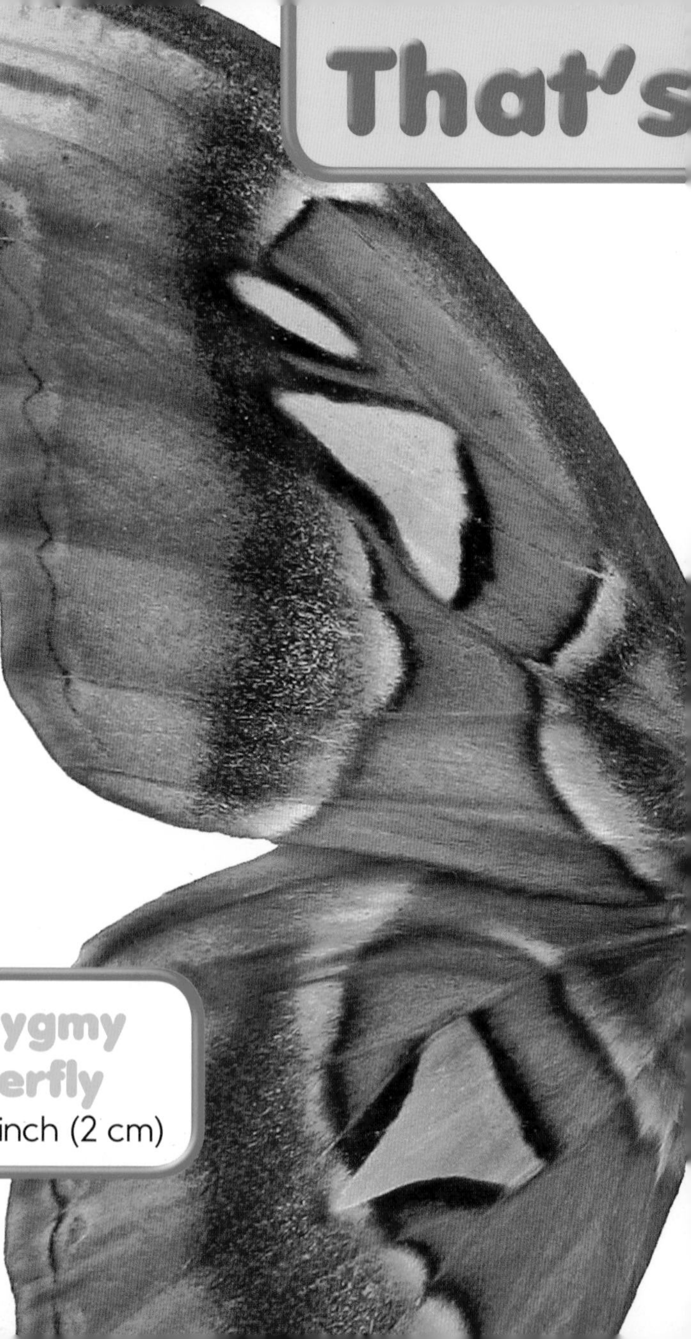

Meet the world's biggest moth and smallest butterfly. They are shown here at their actual sizes!

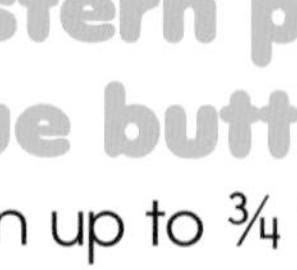

western pygmy
blue butterfly
wingspan up to ¾ inch (2 cm)

Amazing!

giant Atlas moth
wingspan more than 12 inches (30 cm)

Guess Who?

✓ My wings are brightly colored.
✓ I close my wings when I rest.
✓ I fly during the day.

Am I a butterfly or a moth?

Answer: butterfly

Glossary

antennas (an-TEN-uhs): feelers on the head of an insect

insects (IN-sekts): small animals with three main body parts and six legs

nectar (NEK-tur): sweet liquid that some insects collect from flowers

nocturnal (nok-TUR-nuhl): active at night

Index

Facts for Now

Visit this Scholastic Web site for more information
on butterflies and moths:
www.factsfornow.scholastic.com
Enter the keywords **Butterflies and Moths**

About the Author

Lisa M. Herrington loves writing books about animals for kids.
She lives in Trumbull, Connecticut, with her husband, Ryan, and
daughter, Caroline.